THE BRIDGES OF
CENTRAL PARK

Depicted is an aerial view of Central Park around 1864 looking northwest from the intersection of Fifth Avenue and 59th Street. Visible with assistance are 19 bridges, eight future bridge sites, and three transverse roads, including Driprock Arch, future site of Gapstow Bridge over the pond, future site of Inscope Arch, Greengap Arch to the east of the arsenal, future site of Outset Arch, Center Drive Transverse Road No. 1 Bridge, pedestrian transverse bridge over Transverse Road No. 1, East Drive Transverse Bridge over Transverse Road No. 1, Denesmouth Arch carrying Transverse Road No. 1 just above the arsenal, site of East 65th Street Transverse Road No. 1 Bridge, Marble Arch, Willowdell Arch, Riftstone Arch, Bow Bridge, Terrace Bridge, Winterdale Arch, Trefoil Arch, site of Glade Arch, Greywacke Arch, pedestrian bridge over Transverse Road No. 2, future site of Eaglevale Arch, Ladies Pond Bridge, Balcony Bridge, Bank Rock Bridge, Transverse Road No. 3, sites of Bridge No. 24 and Bridge No. 27, and Gothic Bridge. (Historic image 55031 Martel's New York Central Park, 1864 by J. C. Geissler, Lithographer, courtesy I. N. Phelps Stokes Collection, Humanities and Social Science Library, Print Collection, Miriam and Ira D. Wallach Division of Art, Prints and Photographs, The New York Public Library, Astor, Lenox and Tilden Foundations.)

THE BRIDGES OF
CENTRAL PARK

Jennifer C. Spiegler and Paul M. Gaykowski

Copyright © 2006 by Jennifer C. Spiegler and Paul M. Gaykowski
ISBN 0-7385-3861-2

Library of Congress control number: 2005925729

Published by Arcadia Publishing
Charleston SC, Chicago IL, Portsmouth NH, San Francisco CA

Printed in the United States of America

For all general information contact Arcadia Publishing at:
Telephone 843-853-2070
Fax 843-853-0044
E-mail sales@arcadiapublishing.com
For customer service and orders:
Toll-Free 1-888-313-2665

Visit us on the Internet at www.arcadiapublishing.com

CONTENTS

Park bridges alleviate traffic woes. The busy intersection of Center Drive, East Drive, Transverse Road No. 1 and its two bridges, and several pedestrian paths and the bridle trail, skirting the scene, all converge at the entrance to the formal gardens of the mall and Poet's Walk. Marble Arch, Bridge No. 9, safely allows horse and carriage to cross over free from strolling traffic to the mall at the top of the grand marble steps rising out of the ground. Marble Arch was demolished during the overwhelming introduction of the modern automobile on the parkscape. (Enlargement of historic image 55031 Martel's New York Central Park, 1864 by J. C. Geissler, Lithographer, courtesy I. N. Phelps Stokes Collection, Humanities and Social Science Library, Print Collection, Miriam and Ira D. Wallach Division of Art, Prints and Photographs, The New York Public Library, Astor, Lenox and Tilden Foundations.)

ACKNOWLEDGMENTS

The authors wish to express their sincere appreciation to those who helped create this photographic journey over and under *The Bridges of Central Park*. Many terrific people lent their invaluable time and assistance in the realms of research, administration, and perspective.

Research assistance was provided by John Mattera of the New York City Department of Parks and Recreation Library; Sony Onishi, parks photo archivist, New York City Department of Parks and Recreation Photo Archive; Sarah Cedar Miller, historian and photographer of the Central Park Conservancy; David Lowe, photography specialist, the New York Public Library; Melanie Bower, manager of collections access, Museum of the City of New York; Kristine Paulus, reference librarian, Department of Prints, Photographs and Architectural Collections, the New-York Historical Society; and Kitty Chibnik, associate director, Avery Architectural and Fine Arts Library, Columbia University. Those along with many others should know of the deep appreciation afforded.

Important administrative details were provided by Thomas Lisanti and S. Saks, both of Photographic Services and Permissions, the New York Public Library; Jill Reichenbach, rights and reproductions coordinator, the New-York Historical Society; and Marguerite Lavin, Department of Rights and Reproductions, the Museum of the City of New York, among the countless others supporting their fine efforts.

A huge thanks to our supportive friends and family who faithfully provided their opinions, advice, and a keen eye; to wit, we extend our humble gratitude—especially to Stephanie and Arlene.

A clearer perspective was frequently found in conversations with many of the aforementioned individuals.

Most importantly, we are grateful to the New York City Department of Parks and Recreation and their private, nonprofit partner, the Central Park Conservancy, for maintaining Central Park and its structures—especially the bridges.

Historic images referenced to the New York Public Library are credited to the Robert N. Dennis Collection of Stereoscopic Views, Miriam and Ira D. Wallach Division of Art, Prints and Photographs, the New York Public Library, Astor, Lenox and Tilden Foundations.

Historic images referenced to the New-York Historical Society and Museum of the City of New York are identified and credited throughout the text.

Historic images referenced to the New York City Parks and Recreation Library were photographed by the authors from the pages of the recently preserved Central Park Annual Reports collection.

Modern images appearing throughout are from the authors' extensive study and collection of original photography on the subject from 1995 to present.

INTRODUCTION

Meandering Central Park along entwined paths, carriage ways, bridle trails, and crosstown transverses, unique and pleasing landscapes blend together in a kaleidoscope with each step. The seemingly simple yet intricate transportation system incorporates a series of ornate bridges developed to provide free and safe passage for pedestrians, horse-drawn carriages, equestrians, and city traffic alike. Bridges initially designed to elegantly move the masses along separate routes of visual intrigue so as to increase enjoyment and safety for all suddenly became tools of the rapidly emerging profession of the late-1850s American landscape architect responsible for crafting the lush pastoral scenes seen throughout the park today.

New York City park planners of the 1850s had much on their minds aside from ornamental bridges. The natural countryside found in the central and northern climbs of Manhattan Island were disappearing at an alarming rate as the city's population tripled in the 50 years since 1795. The entire island became caged in a grid of streets and avenues newly imposed by lawmakers in Albany that efficiently encouraged growth but perhaps left its citizens feeling claustrophobic. Open spaces were curiously omitted from the grid as "those large arms of the sea," referring to the mighty Hudson and East Rivers, "which embrace Manhattan island" were believed sufficient for health and recreation. Manhattan had just a few bridges along its northern shores connected to the mainland for easy escape to the countryside while the hardships of a thriving industrial revolution took a heavy toll on its citizens.

A grand open space was sorely desired by city dwellers accustomed to seeking recreation in vastly overcrowded private parks and public cemeteries, which provided parklike settings until they began filling with headstones.

An influential editor of the *New York Evening Post*, William Cullen Bryant (1794–1878), in 1845 reflected popular sentiment in his writings regarding the lack of recreational space throughout the city. He called for action on creating a public park to alleviate the "corrupt atmosphere generated in hot and crowded streets." The mostly unoccupied lands of central Manhattan were suggested as a suitable location. Conceived as an antidote to corrupt city life, Central Park soon turned the heads of Europeans and New Yorkers alike.

Following an extensive search for a palatable location, with much consideration given to current land owners, the area chosen with little perceived value at the time was between 59th and 106th Streets (quickly extended to 110th Street) and between Fifth and Eighth Avenues. The park had original boundaries lying exactly five miles from the most northern and southern extremities of Manhattan and about a mile inland on either side, helping derive its seemingly generic name, Central Park.

"The formation of a Public Park, that shall be the ornament of the metropolis of the country, the pride of the State; a trophy of the present for future generations of the patriotism and liberality of the people, and the embodiment of the refined taste and natural science of the age," boasted the *Architects Report* of 1858. "When once the park is opened, and used by the public," the report continued, "the drinking shop and billiard room lose their supremacy. Vice must give way to the pure influence of Nature; and this nature being modified by art will assume its highest and most influential character." The report was signed "Art the Handmaid of Nature."

Architect in chief Frederick Law Olmsted (1822–1903) and consulting architect Calvert Vaux (1824–1895) handcrafted each view in their April 1, 1858, competition-winning design known as Greensward. The initial plan called for merely a handful of inexpensive, simple bridges to fit well within the budget, until a European-influenced Park Board of Commissioners believed Central Park would be nicely suited for well-heeled horseback riders. Architect Jacob Wrey Mould (1825–1886), hired as Vaux's assistant, helped design the additional ornate bridges required to integrate equestrian traffic with pedestrian, carriage, and crosstown traffic patterns while the serenity of the landscape was maintained.

Bridges were first numbered in order of their design sequence and soon co-named with Briticisms such as Dalehead, Gill, and Willowdell, likely inspired by Olmsted's earlier European travels. His observations on traffic difficulties in several major European parks such as Birkenhead Park near Liverpool and the Bois de Boulogne near Paris figured into every aspect of the innovative design, beginning with national pride to unfettered public access. While his democratic notions of a park created for all who could arrive at its gates were noble, the stark reality of the 1800s remained that the bulk of the city's population lacked the resources to make frequent trips north to the park to enjoy its grandeur. The 1858 Greensward blueprint would nevertheless ingeniously transform a one-and-a-third-square-mile swamp otherwise believed to be commercially useless land in the center of the small 33-square-mile Manhattan Island into a revolutionary public park model the world had never seen. Most importantly, its visitors need not be invited aristocrats to enter upon its grounds.

In January 1862, the fifth annual report of the Board of Commissioners of the Central Park classified the bridges into three groups. The purely utilitarian transverse road bridges were built of ordinary stone and brick in a plain manner, devoid of ornament so as to remain inconspicuous objects. Intentionally more visible are the ornamental bridges and arches constructed of similar materials but using selected, usually imported stone and brick. Several were finished with special stone abutments and iron superstructures. Rustic bridges were built chiefly of wood and comprise the smallest class of bridge built in the park.

The following pages highlight the hidden beauty of these massive, practical works of art—the bridges of Central Park. Generally tracing the development of Olmsted and Vaux's original Greensward plan as best as practical, it begins with the first sections to undergo development in the south, addressing each bridge in what is suspected to be the original design sequence number. In many cases, the Central Park Conservancy and park professionals refer to the bridges simply by their numbers rather than the more formal given names.

Today Central Park attracts an estimated 25 million visitors annually and continues its creators' vision of providing a pastoral oasis in the heart of one of the world's largest cities. Its bridges have become models for many modern-day transportation systems in eliminating at-grade crossings. Maintaining the park since 1980 in conjunction with New York City Parks and Recreation is the Central Park Conservancy, a nonprofit organization providing all the basic care and monies through a unique private-public model partnership. Many bridges have been restored and maintained under the conservancy's detailed care.

Readers are encouraged to visit TheBridgesOfCentralPark.com to explore more of the visual study from the authors of *The Bridges of Central Park*.

CENTRAL PARK SOUTH TO TRANSVERSE ROAD NO. 1

The southern reaches of Central Park, featuring the playgrounds, ball grounds, and menagerie, were first to open to a curious general public, most of whom resided a mile or more away below 36th Street. Frequently described as the First Division by early planners, including Frederick Law Olmsted's predecessor and original engineer-in-chief, Egbert L. Viele, the southernmost area was bound by West 59th Street, better known as Central Park South, and the first crosstown transverse at 66th Street, Transverse Road No. 1. Development proceeded in a flurry toward the northern divisions of the park as public demand grew with each added feature announced in the local newspapers. (Historic image courtesy New York City Parks & Recreation Library.)

The original Gapstow Bridge was built by Calvert Vaux and Jacob Wrey Mould in 1874. It served as part of a response to escalating traffic complaints resulting from the wild popularity of park attractions. Southern access paths were simply inundated with foot, carriage, and equestrian traffic streaming north into the park. The landscape architects' office of Frederick Law Olmsted and Vaux suggested three new arches be built to improve traffic flow: Gapstow Bridge over the pond, Outset Arch over the bridle path, and Inscope Arch under the East Drive. The original Gapstow was a unique ornamental suspension-like bridge with decorative cast-iron railings carrying a flat wooden pedestrian path over a narrow neck of the pond. Enduring the elements for about 20 years, it elegantly provided additional access to the promontory peninsula, which is mostly surrounded by the pond. Interestingly, construction of the first Gapstow Bridge was completed during the initial construction phases of another, more famous suspension bridge, the Brooklyn Bridge. (Historic image courtesy The New York Public Library.)

The current massive Manhattan schist stone bridge replacement was designed by Howard and Caudwell in 1896. Built in place of the old wood and iron suspension structure, it continues to grace the northeast neck of the pond. Its graceful curve complements the water and grassy slopes that surround it. During the warm months, ivy, trees, and vines mask the bridge in a green camouflage. Sea grasses bloom from the pond, completely framing the bridge in a deep emerald green. Atop Gapstow Bridge to the south is the impressive modern-day skyline of midtown Manhattan, a view contrary to the original Greensward plan to mask the city from park visitors. Olmsted and Vaux might hardly have imagined the city filling with giant skyscrapers to modern-day heights. Spinning around to the northwest reveals a view of Wollman Rink, which hosts a variety of outdoor activities, including summer carnivals and winter ice-skating. To the west of Gapstow Bridge on the promontory peninsula, the tranquil four-acre Hallett Nature Sanctuary provides a calm, thoughtfully landscaped setting within a block of bustling Fifth Avenue. (Historic image courtesy the Collection of The New-York Historical Society.)

Nestled between a vibrant ice-skating rink, today known as Wollman Rink, and Heckscher Playground, Driprock Arch, Bridge No. 2, carries the Center Carriage Drive north as it jogs around Hallett Nature Sanctuary and the pond. With its massive rock namesake immediately adjacent to this arch, it once provided a right-of-way for horseback riders to reach full gallop on the fairly straight trail above the pond from Greengap Arch. Today it allows pedestrians to pass beneath one of the busiest stretches of carriage drive filled with automobiles, horse-drawn carriages, cyclists, and joggers, as the carriage roads have become a popular exercise course. (Historic image courtesy The New York Public Library.)

Musicians find the acoustical qualities appealing under many of the more substantial stone structures. Perhaps their music is better amplified than playing out in the open air, or they find their audiences more captive to their melodies as they traverse the width of the arcade. In any case, bridges can provide a creative harmonic space and unique sound for those lucky enough to wander into the impromptu theater. Shelter from the elements was an important intended feature of many of the bridges and arches. Long before the city enveloped the park, bridges were among the few man-made structures above midtown Manhattan equally available to the general public for temporary refuge from a sudden rain or snowstorm.

Atop Driprock Arch, Bridge No. 2, Center Drive plays host to an endless cacophony of horse-drawn carriages, automobiles, joggers, cyclists, and charitable event walks. Below Driprock Arch, the former bridle trail provides a soothing alternate scene from the topside activities. The bridges and arches throughout the park were specifically designed to provide a separation of ways. Most were engineered as safety mechanisms to provide different paths for horses and pedestrians to enjoy the park together in harmony. In cases where their uses have been modified, their existences have become much more than a mere separation of ways, but additionally a separation of space. Changing its use from bridle trail crossing to pedestrian crossing, as with most bridges, has opened a new dimension to the park. Events can occur simultaneously above and below the spans in a multitasking fashion.

Details in architecture became hallmarks of Calvert Vaux and Jacob Wrey Mould's bridge designs, frequently to Frederick Law Olmsted's angst at the additional cost. The interior of Driprock Arch, Bridge No. 2, is adorned with square recesses embedded in the red brick ceiling. Sandstone octagonal insets with rosettes are inlaid into the brickwork and flank the arcade entrances.

Driprock Arch was completed in 1859 of red brick with a striking sandstone trim. The substantial arch stands out in a flash of red among the lush greenery that surrounds it. The structure stands 11 feet high and 24 feet long atop the former course of DeVoor's Mill Stream as it ran east toward the pond.

With constant activity on the greens adjacent and atop, Dalehead Arch, Bridge No. 6, allows baseball games and soccer matches to be played uninterrupted while motorists sit in morning rush-hour traffic or as thousands of New York City Marathoners approach the finish line at Tavern on the Green. Built from 1860 to 1862, Dalehead Arch stretches 80 feet long and 24 feet wide, with a height of 11 feet. This elliptical arch was formed of sandstone with quatrefoil cutouts along the balustrade. It has allowed the equestrian trail easy passage for over a century from the playgrounds to the outer bridle trail along Central Park West. DeVoor's Mill Stream once entered the park around West 65th Street and Central Park West and ran to where Dalehead Arch now stands. (Historic image courtesy The New York Public Library.)

Separating more than just ways, Dalehead Arch, Bridge No. 6, provides a gateway from the serene to the bustling ball fields along the bridle trail. On a warm summer night, the many ball fields can be found full of competitive and lighthearted ball games alike. Cheers from the fans in the grandstands can be heard echoing through the arch. Adorning the ceiling of the overpass are several details that make this arcade unique, including concentrically recessed squares in the brickwork on the ceiling and sidewalls. Slightly to the north lies the popular Sheep Meadow, a 15-acre lush green pasture for playing catch, sunbathing, and reading, all while taking in the awesome skyline of midtown Manhattan. Before New Yorkers inherited the meadow, it was home to an actual flock of sheep beginning in 1864. When the sheep were not grazing in the meadow, they were housed in what is now the famous Tavern on the Green restaurant. The sheep were moved to Prospect Park in Brooklyn due to plans to install an aquarium in the future restaurant.

Highly detailed lithograph drawings of the bridges and arches frequently adorned the pages of the Central Park annual reports. Some would have the distinct honor of being reprinted for several consecutive years as chapter cover pages or decorative inside cover artwork. Notably the images would almost universally depict the bridge in a mature landscape, with full-grown trees and plantings much as if the artist had viewed them today rather than before they were actually constructed. Perhaps the detailed renderings are a testament to the high degree of care Calvert Vaux and Jacob Wrey Mould asserted with their work. A true passion for the park in all its virtue is consistently evident from the earliest legislative efforts at the state level, setting aside land through to current-day conservation efforts by the Central Park Conservancy. Interest has yet to wane during the more than 150 years of Central Park in documenting the finer details of its urban renewal and evolution. (Historic image courtesy New York City Parks & Recreation Library.)

Morning, noon, and night, the park canvas changes with each tick of the clock. Morning and afternoon sunshine streaming across the park, unfettered by skyscrapers, has the power to virtually re-create the amazingly detailed balustrade designs on the carriage drives, bridle trail, walking paths, and well-manicured lawns. The fleeting phenomenon is witnessed by only a lucky few who get to enjoy their daily commute with a stroll through the park. City and suburban commuter congestion are all but a surreal traffic report to those traveling between home and work through the heart of this grand urban oasis.

Greengap Arch, Bridge No. 11, was built in clear view of the arsenal, the second-oldest structure in the park. The arsenal was once clearly visible through its arch. Greengap Arch, completed in 1851, was designed to carry a large volume of pedestrians and horse-drawn carriages from Scholar's Gate at 60th Street safely above the busy bridle trail. The arsenal has housed a state munitions depot, the original American Museum of Natural History, and a variety of park and city administrative offices throughout the years. Supporting the 81-foot-wide East Drive and flanking parallel footpaths, Greengap Arch acts as a natural boundary for the Central Park Wildlife Center. Its western arch appears mysteriously gated, providing the wildlife center with a secure perimeter and additional storage within the arcade below. The oldest structure in the park, surpassing the arsenal in age, is Blockhouse No. 1, dating from the War of 1812. It is situated high atop the cliff in the northwestern heights of the park. (Historic image courtesy The New York Public Library.)

Since 1861, a steady stream of horse-drawn carriages has paraded over Greengap Arch along East Drive past the arsenal. Equestrians once galloped below the arch along the bridle trail, situated between Driprock Arch and the now removed Outset Arch. Travelers heading north toward the dignified Poet's Walk might first find themselves diverted with a smart ice-skating lesson at Wollman Rink or a quick visit to their favorite polar bear at the Central Park Wildlife Center, once known as the menagerie with a small collection of animals for children to pet. Polar bears, penguins, monkeys, and sea lions, among other wildlife, now reside at this posh Fifth Avenue address. The walkway under the arch closed to pedestrians in 1988 during wildlife center renovations, making the East Drive and Greengap Arch a natural boundary. With a long 81-foot underpass to accommodate the traffic volume overhead, the span measures only 25 feet wide. It is made of Alberta sandstone set in ashlar.

Taking the West Drive over a pedestrian path east of West 61st Street, Greyshot Arch, Bridge No. 13, is located just north of Merchants Gate at Columbus Circle. Constructed from 1860 to 1862, this arch supports bikers, skaters, marathoners, automobiles, and horse-drawn carriage traffic near the elegant Tavern on the Green restaurant. The casual stroller remains insulated from the bustle of busy West Drive by simply meandering through its 30-foot-six-inch-wide arch lined with pressed Philadelphia red brick. Westchester County gneiss, a grayish stone with hints of dark orange, lends a subtle color tone to the span. It stands just over 10 feet high. (Historic image courtesy The New York Public Library.)

This part of the park near the busy southwest corner of 59th Street and Central Park West was identified as a priority for early construction efforts due to its proximity to Manhattan's rapidly expanding northbound population. Through Greyshot Arch, pedestrians can easily access interior park areas without having to cross the West Drive carriage road. This busy southern section of the park contains a high density of bridges and arches as much activity and congestion was anticipated by Frederick Law Olmsted and Calvert Vaux. True to their

vision, Columbus Circle still buzzes with activity less than a city block away from Greyshot Arch. Touching the park, Broadway provides a constant stream of park visitors, throwing open the gates to anyone who could board any of its reasonably priced streetcars, trolleys, trains, or buses. Pedestrians strolling over the arch may notice the detailed fleur-de-lis pattern in each balustrade. This delicate, repetitive carved-stone design runs the entire length of the bridge.

Children of all ages may be seen running through Playmates Arch, Bridge No. 14, beneath the bustling Center Drive carriage road between the dairy, Chess and Checkers House, and the carousel. Playmates Arch carries Center Drive north toward Transverse Road No. 1 at 66th Street, just a few feet away. Frederick Law Olmsted playfully named this area of the park the Children's District, a reason why the arch received its name. The district entailed the dairy, the Kinderberg, a rustic shelter replaced by the Chess and Checkers House, a children's cottage with live animals, and the carousel. (Historic image courtesy The New York Public Library.)

Children are particularly well served by Playmates Arch as they dash beneath the bustling Center Drive along the length of its 66-foot arcade. The lengthy underpass probably seems a bit too long for most children who spy the carousel in the distance. The carousel is constructed in a similar stone and style design as Playmates Arch. It has been storied that a blind mule and horse below the floor operated the original carousel around 1871. Two other steam-powered carousels came into play but were destroyed by fires. Today the fourth carousel at this site is among the largest in the United States, with 58 hand-carved, painted horses.

As with many of the bridges and arches carrying the drives around the park, they play a significant role in allowing discordant events to occur simultaneously. Charity walks continue undisturbed along Center Drive while restless children hurry between the Kinderberg, carousel, ball grounds, and dairy. The dairy once served refreshments of fresh milk and was considered alone an important health reason to visit the park on a regular basis. Fresh dairy products increasingly became a difficult commodity to find on Manhattan Island as the city rapidly swept over its northern farming communities, fueled in part by the sheer existence of the park itself. In the effort to provide healthy and essential dairy products, the park retained small numbers of farm animals to mimic a rural farm setting that was quickly vanishing. Today the dairy serves as an information center and official Central Park gift shop. (Historic image courtesy The New York Public Library.)

Details rarely escaped Calvert Vaux and Jacob Wrey Mould's attention. The striking contrast of pressed Philadelphia red brick and Milwaukee white brick lends a unique visual experience to Playmates Arch, especially in the long arcade below. Achieving such a striking visual result with the permanency of the actual construction materials ensures an enduring original design that remains long after construction. Each interior red brick was meticulously set on its edge width-wise in single 66-foot-long rows. Directly in opposition in both color and form are alternating rows of four white brick groups. This three-dimensional brickwork concept creates a design that could hardly be mimicked by the use of traditional decorative substances such as paint.

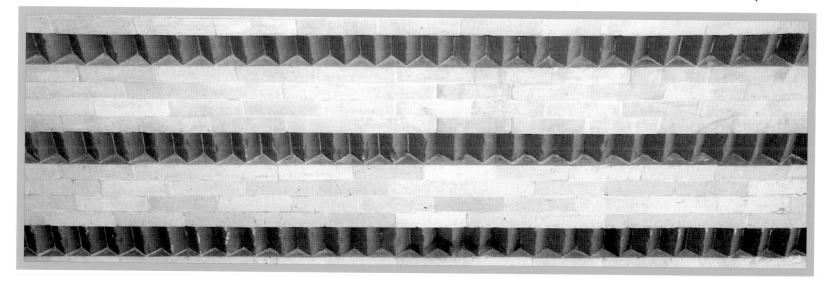

Horses and carriages continue to cross Playmates Arch throughout its history. Designed by Calvert Vaux and Jacob Wrey Mould, Playmates Arch was built in 1863 of pressed Philadelphia red brick with Milwaukee white brick-belt coursing and granite trim. The nearby carousel and Chess and Checkers House buildings were constructed in a similar stone and design style as Playmates Arch, lending a common visual continuity among all three structures. In 1989, the Central Park Conservancy and the New York City Department of Parks and Recreation restored and replaced much of the cast-iron railings and balustrades along Playmates Arch. (Historic image courtesy New York City Parks & Recreation Library.)

Hidden among the pines in lower southwest Central Park, this elegant cast-iron bridge allows equestrians riding the bridle trail to pass through a ravine lined with solid rock. Pinebank Arch, Bridge No. 15, is a graceful structure surrounded by many heavily traversed areas, including Columbus Circle, Heckscher Playground, and the Maine Monument. Located east of the West Drive at 62nd Street, it was constructed in 1861 by Calvert Vaux and J. B. and W. W. Cornell Ironworks. (Historic image courtesy The New York Public Library.)

The sole survivor among three original cast-iron bridges that spanned the bridle trail in the southern First District of the park, Pinebank Arch allows unfettered access for eager children running toward the playgrounds and ball fields. Mid-span and along the adjacent gently sloping rocks, great views are available each autumn of excited marathoners giving it their best while crossing Greyshot Arch on West Drive during the final quarter mile of the New York City Marathon.

Many of the more-than-a-century-old bridges and arches of Central Park have required extensive restoration work at various periods due to both age and vandalism. The *New York Times* reported that Pinebank Arch underwent an extensive restoration during much of 1984. Its cast-iron superstructure had begun to rust badly. Whole pieces of the ornamental handrails and balustrades were entirely missing altogether. The New York City Department of Parks and Recreation hired an architectural firm with expertise in restoration to conduct a $300,000 reconstruction of the arch. The entire length of the structural arch was sandblasted and corroded sections were replaced. Missing parts were fabricated and structural cast-iron segments were reassembled and painted. The concrete deck was replaced with wood. Brand-new ornamental sections were cast in the likeness of the original design. (Historic image courtesy the Collection of The New-York Historical Society.)

Basking in the glow of the skyscrapers towering over Columbus Circle on a clear winter evening, the grounds surrounding Pinebank Arch, including Heckscher Playground, the ball grounds, and the bridle trail, received extensive renovations in 2006 under the watchful care of the Central Park Conservancy. The southernmost bridle trail terminus received a proper turnaround area so horseback riders have ample space to turn and head north. Pinebank Arch has become the final bridge an equestrian has the distinct pleasure of passing beneath while riding south. The bridle trail once continued east under the now-removed Spur Rock Arch, through Driprock Arch, beneath the gated Greengap Arch, and around a bend south under the removed Outset Arch.

Providing a clear, unobstructed path from the midtown entrance of the park at Seventh Avenue and Central Park South straight into Heckscher Playground, Dipway Arch, Bridge No. 16, allows visitors to dip below the busy South Drive carriage way. Exiting to the north from under this hillside-embedded arch, the pedestrian path meanders past Spur Rock, the former site of the elegant cast-iron Spur Rock Arch. (Historic image courtesy The New York Public Library.)

Most of the bridges and arches carrying the circuitous carriage drives continue to perform the tasks exactly as they were designed. Elegant horse-drawn carriages make their usual rounds trotting across many of the stately park bridges of the lower First Division. Below Dipway Arch, stylish "ladies seats" provided cool relief from the blistering sun intended for women and children of the 19th century alike. Beneath the masonry with its natural cooling properties, women and children were able to rest in the shade of the arch while the men of the age took part in what was thought to be more strenuous activities elsewhere in the park. Each seat, framed with a nicely detailed arch, was seemingly large enough for a woman's hoopskirt and perhaps her child in tow.

Archways throughout the park clearly provided a necessary function of an early system of shelters. Affording options to take cover wherever one of the many substantial bridges were found, visitors were able to duck away from nature's wrath including rain, lightning, and snowstorms. Dipway Arch appears deceptively compact in form. Its arch stands 11.5 feet high with 15.5 feet between abutments. Its giant curved flanking stone buttresses, however, measuring 150 feet and 9 inches long, lend it the title of the largest bridge in overall extreme breadth anywhere in the park. Dipway Arch was renovated in 1996 by the Central Park Conservancy. (Historic image courtesy The New York Public Library.)

Hidden and hard to find, yet located in one of the most heavily traveled sections of the park, Inscope Arch, Bridge No. 33, carries the southeastern beginnings of the East Drive from Grand Army Plaza north toward the mall. It was designed to accommodate only foot traffic below. Constructed in 1875, a relative latecomer, Bridge No. 33 was built in response to increasing traffic congestion near a popular point of entry, Scholar's Gate. The crush of pedestrians, horseback riders, and carriage drivers caused bottleneck situations that irritated all. The Department of Public Parks needed a remedy. The landscape architects' office of Frederick Law Olmsted and Calvert Vaux suggested three new arches be built to improve traffic flow: Gapstow Bridge over the pond, Outset Arch over the bridle path, and Inscope Arch beneath East Drive. All were designed specifically to safely reroute pedestrian traffic. A challenge to construct, the site of Inscope Arch was once a swamp through which DeVoor's Mill Stream trickled. The cost to create this arch was higher than similar construction during Civil War days. Inscope stands at 12 feet and is 13 feet and seven inches long. (Historic image courtesy New York Public Library.)

Inscope Arch was part of a large restoration plan conducted by the Central Park Conservancy beginning in 2000, encompassing a huge section of the southeast area of the park. While the restoration focused on the 11.5 acres surrounding the pond, Inscope Arch's stone was cleaned, the interior was painted, and lights were repaired inside the 34-foot passageway.

Inscope Arch was designed absent a traditional balustrade. Instead it was smartly planted across its span along the wide grassy swaths flanking the East Drive and the parallel paths above. "Central Park was found in a 'tangled and trackless waste' but was left as a landscaped garden of unsurpassed beauty," an 1871 article in the *New York Times* pointed out. (Historic image courtesy the Collection of The New-York Historical Society.)

TRANSVERSE ROAD NO. 1 TO TERRACE DRIVE

The mall was one of the first areas of the park to be designed. Created as a wide, direct pedestrian route lined with American elms, it sometimes was referred to as the promenade or the avenue. Positioned on a diagonal aligned to true north, it extended a quarter of a mile from Transverse Road No. 1 at 65th Street (near Marble Arch) to Terrace Road at 72nd Street. Leading the visitor from the Fifth Avenue entrance at 59th Street to the heart of the park via the most direct route, the mall served as an elegant public meeting place. New York City park planners felt a need to include a sociable promenade similar to those found in major European metropolises. (Historic image courtesy New York City Parks & Recreation Library.)

Considered a crowning architectural achievement of Frederick Law Olmsted's Greensward plan, Bethesda Terrace, including the Terrace Bridge, was designed and constructed by Calvert Vaux and Jacob Wrey Mould from 1859 to 1869. It defined the heart of the park as it joined the formal mall to the reflective lake, overlooking the wild ramble and beyond to a distant vista. Terrace Bridge helps connect East Drive and West Drive via Terrace Road—essentially a rough through-park extension of West 72nd Street that crosses the bridge. (Historic image courtesy The New-York Historical Society.)

Terrace Road was considered an alternate type of surface transverse road. It could be open to crosstown traffic during daylight hours to relieve congestion along the four sunken transverse roads, which were thought generally sufficient for round-the-clock use. Built of New Brunswick sandstone and granite in a mixture of Romanesque, Gothic, and classical styles, Mould executed the detailed work on the stone lining the grand staircases that descend to Bethesda Fountain. The several steps at the shoreline beyond the fountain lead into the lake and were once a boarding location for guide boats.

Meticulous sandstone carvings completely adorn the Terrace Bridge, Bridge No. 1. They depict incredibly detailed scenes celebrating nature's great agricultural bounty. The seasons are marked with stone-carved dioramas, including a witch soaring on her broomstick over a jack-o'-lantern. Scenes portray nighttime with a lamp and book, and a bat and an owl, and daytime with a rising sun and a crowing rooster. Fish, game, and beekeepers, among other agricultural scenes, adorn various portions of the sprawling balustrade, marking a time when farming was an important focus of New York City's economy. Energy reverberates among the spontaneous gatherings as musicians, actors, and dancers enchant the curious crowds. Performers frequently use the cavernous arcade beneath the bridge to their advantage as an impromptu theater. The Victorian encaustic tile ceiling of the Terrace Bridge arcade, first installed in 1867, was covered with nearly 16,000 tiles, weighing about 50 tons. Commonly called the Minton tile ceiling, named after its British manufacturer, the vivid colorful tiles depicted a floral design shiny enough to illuminate the arcade with the available natural light. Restoration and a long-term maintenance effort have been underway by the Central Park Conservancy to repair damage that has been sustained by Terrace Bridge over the years. The Minton tiles were the only known Victorian encaustic ceiling tile installation in the world until 1983.

The strikingly formal design of Terrace Bridge and its immediate surroundings reflects a common tendency of a young nation to emulate its European origins. This Old World throwback lures park visitors from the southernmost reaches of the mall directly true north to the shores of the refreshing lake by way of a vista point. Belvedere Castle, just north of the wild ramble and across Transverse No. 2, was the intended, seemingly elusive destination. The castle was to be the only man-made structure obviously visible within the park. Many European parks were designed with faux castles intended simply to guide the curious through a well-manicured, controlled experience. The combination of the mall, Terrace Bridge, and Belvedere Castle worked together as one expansive formal feature, where natural beauty was primary. These three elements separately viewed in their local surroundings could hardly reveal their embedded, larger purpose. (Historic image courtesy New York City Parks & Recreation Library.)

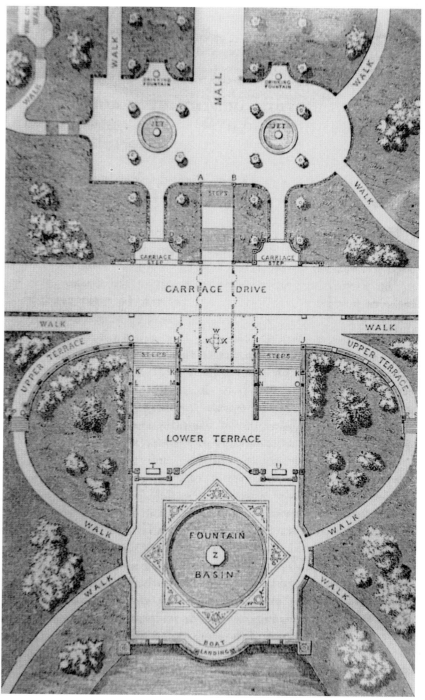

Bethesda Fountain, with its well-known sculpture *Angel of Waters*, heralded the opening of the Croton Aqueduct in 1842, allowing clean drinking water to flow into the Croton Reservoir, now the Great Lawn. Powered directly from the aqueduct, the fountain was a symbol of quality drinking water the city desperately needed. Pioneering artist Emma Stebbins received the commission, the only sculpture requested for the park during its early development. The *New York Times* published in 1873, "The park embodies so many attractions and conveniences within its boundaries, affording opportunities for instruction, amusement, and improvement of both the minds and bodies . . . while at the same time a beautiful garden and pleasure-ground is here provided . . . through off the weariness and monotony produced by over application to daily labor . . . their minds may be diverted from the troubles of everyday life in the contemplation of the beauties of nature and hart here so wonderfully combined." (Historic image courtesy The New York Public Library.)

Built in 1861 by Calvert Vaux and Jacob Wrey Mould, Willowdell Arch, Bridge No. 3, carries East Drive northbound over a pedestrian path linking the mall with the dene. Willowdell Arch is made of red brick and sandstone. The original cast-iron railing was replaced with wood. Willowdell Arch straddles an old streambed that drained the mall area and fed DeVoor's Mill Stream. Frederick Law Olmsted and Vaux devised a system of drives, footpaths, and bridle paths that would create a separation of ways similar to transverse roads serving the same purpose. Those strolling under the Willowdell Arch would never cross the busy carriage drive traffic. This circulation system ensured that the visitor's use of the park would be carefree. (Historic image courtesy The New York Public Library.)

Park visitors could sit on the ladies seats inside Willowdell's 14-foot-10-inch-wide arch and rest in the cool shade with their children. Remnants of a drinking fountain remain nestled along the north side of the arcade, embedded in the center bench recess. Thirsty visitors returning from the mall would have certainly made this arch a destination for both refreshment and relaxation. As a thoroughfare, the mall had numerous walkways separated by trees and lawns. In the mid-1860s, the parkway idea Frederick Law Olmsted and Calvert Vaux introduced into American city planning became a phenomenon. These wide residential avenues allowed vehicles, horseback riders, and pedestrians to keep their own lanes, separated by strips of grass and rows of trees similar to the format found at the mall. They constructed the first parkway in Buffalo from 1868 to 1870 and then proposed their new type of passageway in Chicago, a link to the new suburb of Riverside. A parkway for Brooklyn, connecting Prospect Park to the beaches of the Atlantic Ocean, was next in line. The experience with the mall evidently trained their thinking on the form and design of these innovative roadways. (Historic image courtesy The New York Public Library.)

At the eastern entrance to Willowdell Arch stands a bronze sculpture of a dog named Balto. He represents the efforts of Alaskan sled dogs that transported medication across Alaska. An inscription commemorating Balto reads, "Dedicated to the indomitable spirit of the sled dog that relayed antitoxin six hundred miles over rough ice across treacherous waters through arctic blizzards from Nenana to the relief of stricken Nome in the winter of 1925. Endurance. Fidelity. Intelligence."

Among Calvert Vaux's earliest bridges, constructed from 1859 to 1860, Denesmouth Arch, Bridge No. 7, is an anomaly designed to carry crosstown traffic along Transverse Road No. 1 above ground rather than below the grade of enjoyable parklands. It permits north-south pedestrian traffic to stylishly pass under a chaotic vein of unimpeded city traffic between the rolling dene and the menagerie, an early predecessor of the Central Park Wildlife Center. A constant flow of city buses, taxis, trucks, and private automobiles may be found atop this transverse at anytime of the day or night as they make their way east along 65th Street. Below, this massive arch serves as only one of two passageways to the Children's Zoo. The adjacent Delacorte Musical Clock Tower can be heard striking a familiar nursery rhyme on the half hour. A bronze marching band of animal figurines dance around the clock tower in step while playing their musical instruments. (Historic image courtesy The New York Public Library.)

Made of light brown New Brunswick sandstone, Denesmouth Arch stands over 37 feet long and 14 feet high. It is the only bridge made entirely of sandstone. Notable is the Gothic detail in the quatrefoil circles flanking each side of the arch. The arch was built above a former streambed that originated from the mall and snaked through the Central Park Wildlife Center toward Inscope Arch. Originally, the railing atop the bridge had four large posts, with ornate, elegantly designed lamps. Only one survived and is currently in storage. Denesmouth Arch once carried traffic in both east and west directions. Today's modern one-way system of streets has left it carrying only eastbound traffic. (Historic image courtesy New York City Parks & Recreation Library.)

Built to better connect Manhattan's one-way street grid with Transverse Road No. 1 at East 66th Street, this modern extension is constructed over the same streambed as its more elegant neighbor, Denesmouth Arch. The East 65th Street Transverse Bridge (westbound) is one of only three raised transverse crossings in the entire park, all of which are part of Transverse Road No. 1. The underpass serves as a natural meeting point for those eager to feed the animals at the Children's Zoo and view the ever-popular polar bears at the Central Park Wildlife Center. Just to its north lies the dene, a hilly area of large bare rock that once channeled an ancient tributary of DeVoor's Mill Stream within its valley.

Built over the rather extensive former DeVoor's Mill Stream as it entered the park, West 65th Street Transverse Bridge (eastbound) allows one-way traffic entering at West 65th Street to merge into the two-way traffic pattern of Transverse Road No. 1. This bridge rests just south of Tavern on the Green and southwest of Sheep Meadow. Overhead, it provides an excellent vantage point for viewing the Macy's Thanksgiving Day parade balloons as they glide down Central Park West. Below the span provides separate paths for horses to trot and pedestrians to meander.

Frederick Law Olmsted once observed, "The time will come when New York will be built up, when all the grading and filling will be done, and when the picturesquely varied, rocky formations of the Island will have been converted into formations for rows of monotonous straight streets, and piles of erect buildings. There will be no suggestion left of its present varied surface, with the single exception of the few acres contained in the park. Then the priceless value of the present picturesque outlines of the ground will be perceived, and its adaptability for its purpose more fully recognized."

Frederick Law Olmsted and Calvert Vaux's sunken transverse roads were among the most unique and innovative design aspects of their Greensward plan. Transverse Road No. 1 allowed for unimpeded crosstown traffic flow and was a mandatory element of the design competition as set forth by the park board under the requirements of the state law that established the park boundaries. The Greensward plan created four recessed crosstown roads or transverses to link the everyday commerce of the Upper East and Upper West Side neighborhoods of Manhattan even though New York's population center remained a few miles south of the park's southernmost border. These roads divided the park into five sections that spurred various styles of landscape design. The sunken transverse concept developed around the time when the world had just begun looking toward transportation on a subterranean level as London's Underground was rushing to fruition. (Historic image courtesy New York City Parks & Recreation Library.)

Located at a passage to Strawberry Fields, Riftstone Arch, Bridge No. 18, guides tourists, walking commuters, and automobile traffic from West 72nd Street seamlessly over the bridle path to the West Drive. Completed in 1861, this rustic stone arch is constructed of solid, colorful rubble stone quarried from the immediate vicinity in a cost-cutting effort. The rustic stone arch stands 11 feet nine inches high and 30 feet long. The terrain surrounding Riftstone Arch gently slopes down to the bridle path along dirt trails obscured by shrubs, boulders, and colorful flowerbeds. Its supporting walls remain unnoticed, providing a feeling of natural passage through the excavated valley below. When park drives are open, Riftstone Arch carries both east and westbound automobile traffic for ease in entering and exiting the park at West 72nd Street. Yet, beneath the nearly invisible Riftstone Arch, equestrians and joggers go about their activities unaware of the crowds above.

Riftstone Arch is one of the few arches absent a balustrade, making the bridge practically invisible to its topside visitors. Busloads of tourists regularly disembark to take photographs of the Dakota Apartments and gather atop the arch, which is level and nearly indistinguishable from Central Park West. Visitors can join the residents of Central Park West from this prime location to welcome the annual Macy's Thanksgiving Day parade.

A bridge lost to the forces of change in the big city, Marble Arch succumbed to the demands of 20th-century automobile traffic. It was demolished in 1938. This unique arch created of pure marble contained two rows of ladies seats and a stylized drinking fountain that provided shade, shelter, and refreshment. Designed as an entrance to the mall, the arch drew pedestrians from the Children's District over a small footbridge spanning Transverse Road No. 1. Clarence Cook wrote of this graceful, restful underpass in 1869, "This is one of the pleasantest and most elegantly built of all these cool places for rest and refreshment. It is entered at one end of a level with a foot path; at the other a double stairway to the left and right leads to the level of the Mall and to the carriage-road which this archway is designed to carry. It is called the marble archway to distinguish it, all other structures of this sort in the Park being built either of stone, or brick, or of brick and stone combined. The marble employed is the coarse limestone from the Westchester quarries . . . A marble bench runs along each side, and at the end." (Historic image courtesy The New York Public Library.)

CHAPTER

TERRACE DRIVE
TO TRANSVERSE ROAD NO. 2

Carved from the swampy remnants of the south branch of the Saw Kill stream, the 18-acre lake provided convenient skating and boating exercise for park visitors. The glistening lake was designed to reflect the shores of its whimsical northern neighbor, the lush wooded forest of the ramble. Together they create a vast tranquil haven for resident wildlife, migratory birds, and nature enthusiasts. The combined 56-acre canvas is neatly nestled between Terrace Drive at 72nd Street north to Transverse Road No. 2 at 79th Street and the East and West Carriage Drives. (Historic image courtesy New York City Parks & Recreation Library.)

Just east of the American Museum of Natural History, hidden in marshland, stands Balcony Bridge, Bridge No. 4. Constructed in 1860 of Manhattan schist excavated from the park and mountain greywacke, this 27-foot span carries West Drive traffic over a now small tributary stream. In the 1870s, this stream linked the lake with a small body of water to the west known as Ladies Pond. The stream was both wide and deep enough to allow rowboats to venture beneath Balcony Bridge into a deep rock-walled ravine toward rustic wooden Bridge No. 22 (frequently referred to as Ladies Pond Bridge). Ladies Pond was backfilled in the 1930s, and the water below the bridge became a natural marsh swamp, a mere vestige of itself. (Historic image courtesy The New York Public Library.)

Bird-watchers have enjoyed scenes of the ramble and its wildlife from atop Balcony Bridge for more than a century and a half. Eastern views abound of well-managed natural settings such as the lake, the Hernshead peninsula, and the ramble from either of the two balconies protruding from the eastern balustrade. Balconies are notably absent from the western balustrade, a rare original asymmetric design distinction shared only with Trefoil Arch on the eastern side of the lake. City views were originally obscured with lush plantings around the perimeter of the park by intentional design to "plant-out" the city. Modern city skyscrapers now tower over the park, bringing well into focus many originally unintended views of exterior man-made objects. This is especially true of many of the highest bridges.

Balcony Bridge has fallen into obscurity as its surroundings have matured and better camouflaged the arch from the causal park observer. Plantings have in fact matured throughout the park, helping better mask these gems of the Greensward plan. Frederick Law Olmsted might be pleased to see his creations succumbing to nature itself. His original plans for most of the bridges and arches were to be low-key, almost invisible man-made structures owing their existence to the mere practicality of safe passage and complete park access. (Historic image courtesy the Collection of The New-York Historical Society.)

Majestically spanning Cherry Hill point and the ramble, this graceful wrought iron bridge was built at great expense with outstanding attention to detail. It elegantly crosses the lake, allowing foot traffic to flow over blissful boaters and sassy swans. Its name derives from its resemblance to the graceful lines of an archer's bow. The Bow Bridge, Bridge No. 5, was constructed between 1859 and 1862 with an 87-foot span. With a two- to three-inch differential in foundation heights, cannonballs were placed under the abutments as movable bearings to allow the bridge to expand and contract with the seasonal temperatures. Due to a natural difference in elevation of the two shorelines, the north abutment rests lower than the south. From center span, one can see both the east and west sides of Manhattan, a unique vantage point. Renting a small rowboat from the Loeb Boathouse on the far eastern shore is an excellent way to explore the lake. (Historic image courtesy the Collection of The New-York Historical Society.)

Calvert Vaux and Jacob Wrey Mould became masters in the advanced art of forging ornate details and traits of cast iron. They used their newfound talents selectively, and Bow Bridge and its surroundings clearly benefited from their choice. The material chosen for the Bow Bridge was indeed cast iron with wooden floors as it provided a "light graceful effect in relation to the lake and the ramble." Originally, eight enormous planting vases were fixed to its abutments, which no longer remain on this classic Greek-style bridge with Gothic cinquefoil designs. (Historic image courtesy The New York Public Library.)

Bow Bridge exhibits cast-iron work similar to that of the dome of the U.S. Capitol. It was "fabricated from the same ironworks." Rededicated on September 23, 1974, following a two-year, $361,000 restoration project, Bow Bridge was reopened to the general public. Two major donors, Lucy G. Moses and Lila Acheson Wallace, received the honor of cutting a ceremonious blue ribbon commemorating the day. Moses said, "I hope people will enjoy it for generations to come."

Several boating services have plied the waters beneath Bow Bridge in the late 19th century, making use of the five landings. "Call" boats could ferry up to six passengers to any of the five boat landings found along the lakeshore. Passage boats could sail with a dozen passengers aboard on scenic tours around the lake. Four of the original boat landings have been restored and augmented with sheltering roofs. Visitors may rent rowboats to explore the secluded coves and romantically drift beneath Bow Bridge at their own pace. (Historic image courtesy the Collection of The New-York Historical Society.)

The *New York Times* reported that some 300 ice-skaters turned up on the unfinished lake on a cold Sunday in December 1858. Rather unceremoniously, they were among the first New Yorkers to play in Central Park, spurring a trend that saw 10,000 take to the ice the following weekend and double that on Christmas Day. Development continued with the public sampling the newest features long before they were completed.

Bow Bridge was one of seven cast-iron bridges built in Central Park from 1859 through 1875. Two were removed under parks commissioner Robert Moses in the 1930s: Spur Rock Arch and Outset Arch. Bow Bridge appears suddenly from the dense foliage of the ramble. (Historic image courtesy the Collection of The New-York Historical Society.)

Due to the exceptional weather on a June day in 1874, the park was full of people strolling the promenade, rambling the pathways, sailing on the lake, and crowding the bridges, the *New York Times* reported. Even a quiet and secluded spot in the ramble, or anywhere, could not be found. "The lake was voered with boats, and the boatmen must have reaped a rich harvest . . . Never did the City's great garden appear to better advantage and so well repay its visitors." (Historic image courtesy the Collection of The New-York Historical Society.)

At the foot of Cedar Hill on the Upper East Side, a popular destination for traditional park activities such as picnics, sunbathing, and reading the *New York Times*, stands the massive ashlar stone structure of Glade Arch, Bridge No. 8. It provides a walkway in a serene setting of rolling inclines among full grown trees. The sweeping hillside of the glade lends itself nicely to a romantic picnic on a summer day or a quick sleigh ride on freshly fallen snow. (Historic image courtesy The New York Public Library.)

Frederick Law Olmsted and Calvert Vaux proved to be a cohesive team of true pioneers in developing the overarching concepts of the great urban American public park, including its function and design. Vaux was singularly responsible for the design of physical structures in the park, including bridges, houses, monuments, and walls. Associate architect Jacob Wrey Mould assisted Vaux in his designs. (Historic image courtesy New York City Parks & Recreation Library.)

Built in 1862, Glade Arch originally supported carriage traffic and a pedestrian path leading to the intersection of Fifth Avenue and 79th Street from the lake area. Constructed with a light-colored New Brunswick sandstone and ashlar, quatrefoil designs and diamond patterns adorn the stonework. Its gradual arch rises only 10 feet in the 29 feet of its span. The arch has retained its width from the days when it carried both a carriage road and footpath. It now appears oversized for its sole purpose of carrying two simple footpaths one over another. Glade Arch has been renovated on several occasions by the Central Park Community Fund, Greensward Foundation, Bankers Trust Company, and the Central Park Conservancy.

This well-hidden wooden footbridge provides a natural haven for bird-watchers on the western edge of the ramble. Bank Rock Bridge, Bridge No. 10, has taken several names during its various reincarnations. Among the more popular names were Oak Bridge, Cabinet Bridge, and Bank Rock Bridge. It provides one of only two over-water entrances to the ramble and is located on the west side at 77th Street. The only other access to the ramble over water is with Bow Bridge to the southeast. (Historic image courtesy The New York Public Library.)

Bank Rock Bridge crosses a narrow inlet of the lake leading to the swampy marsh of Bank Rock Bay, a natural habitat for migratory birds, interesting trees, and a variety of plant life. Akin to the types of boardwalks found along trails in recreational swamplands, Bank Rock Bridge guides visitors through a low marsh camouflage providing a front-row view of wildlife activity. (Historic image courtesy the Collection of TheNew-York Historical Society.)

First constructed in 1860, the previously called Oak Bridge was created of white oak, cast iron, and yellow pine on a stone foundation. It was eventually replaced with spiked steel handrails and a heavier wooden floor to survive the weather and swampy conditions. (Historic image courtesy New York City Parks & Recreation Library.)

Along the park path at 74th Street, under the East Drive near the Loeb Boathouse and the lake, sits Trefoil Arch, Bridge No. 12. The 15-foot-10-inch-long and 11-foot-9-inch-high bridge was constructed in 1862 of brownstone from the banks of the Passaic and Connecticut Rivers. The passageway is 60 feet long and made of brick with a wooden ceiling. (Historic image courtesy The New York Public Library.)

The east side of Trefoil Arch features a large trefoil, a three-clover curved design like a shamrock. The west side of this arch is curved with a round archway of wedge-shaped stones. There is a staircase that heads down to the relatively hidden round archway. This is a favorite spot for performers, as the echo of their song and dance spread up the staircase, which provides ample audience seating. Balcony Bridge shares a similar distinction in that an intentional asymmetric feature is designed into its span. Balcony Bridge contains balconies only on its eastern balustrade.

Quatrefoil design emblems flank the east entrance of Trefoil Arch. At the southern end of the glade, where Trefoil sits, reside the statues of Hans Christian Andersen and Alice in Wonderland. (Historic image courtesy the Collection of The New-York Historical Society.)

Strolling east along the pathway from the terrace along the lake leads to a set of stairs that head down to the round arch. This arch sets the stage as a favorite spot for performers as the echo of their song and dance attract spectators. The Central Park Conservancy restored Trefoil Arch from 1983 to 1985. (Historic image courtesy New York City Parks & Recreation Library.)

Wandering carefree through the ramble, visitors searching for Belvedere Castle might stumble upon the Ramble Stone Arch, Bridge No. 20, nestled deep within. Placed between two massive boulder outcroppings, this 5-foot-narrow, 13.5-foot-tall arch can be found in a tight rocky ravine just around the bend from the original site of the cave. Visitors rambling along the various twisting paths and steep slopes may be lucky to stumble upon its 32-foot-long balustrade spanning the rugged terrain. The rocky, rustic walkway atop the arch blends amazingly well with the surrounding boulders as almost to fool the eye. On approach, the changing visual angles appear to cause the arch to disappear into the rocks flanking and supporting it. Crossing the three-foot-wide path atop the arch can best be enjoyed single file as the arch is quite narrow. The Ramble Stone Arch is well hidden among the maze of paths strewn across the hills and valleys of the western ramble. (Historic image courtesy The New York Public Library.)

In 1991, a *New York Times* article reported that the Ramble Stone Arch resembles "a keyhole through a rocky valley, almost a secret passage to frame an Indiana Jones adventure." Just to the south of the Ramble Stone Arch, a conspicuous cave in the form of a partly man-made structure of rocks was nestled into a rocky alcove of the lake. The profound blocks of fashioned stone, which appear haphazardly constructed, almost defy the imagination. Climbing down an uneven steep stairway carved out of the rock face leads down to the former cave. (Historic image courtesy New York City Parks & Recreation Library.)

A simple wooden bridge spanning the mouth of its namesake stream, Gill Bridge, Bridge No. 21, continues the shoreside path north before climbing into the rocky hills of the ramble. The gill itself is a narrow stream gently cascading into the lake from pools far above. The stream quietly flows beneath the ornamental wooden bridge atop where stunning lakeside views can be savored. The bridge is located on the west side between 75th and 76th Streets, nestled up in a cove across from the Hernshead peninsula. (Historic image courtesy The New York Public Library.)

With its rocky terrain, secluded paths, and tumbling stream, the Gill Bridge provides an explorer with a true discovery tour of a northern woods ravine. (Historic image courtesy The New York Public Library.)

Crossing a narrow stream feeding the lake through a deep ravine, this relatively substantial rustic wooden bridge, Bridge No. 22, once linked two fairly remote necks of land. In the shadows of Balcony Bridge and Eaglevale Arch, Bridge No. 22 provides a connection between two unique landscapes separated by a body of water known as Ladies Pond. The pond was drained and backfilled in the 1930s. A rustic alternative to the massive Balcony Bridge just up the stream, this wooden bridge leads visitors across a deep ravine once transited by rowboats. Naturalists Walk begins just to the north of Bridge No. 22. Central Park Conservancy workers skilled in wood construction fully rebuilt this rustic wooden footbridge in 1996. (Historic image courtesy New York City Parks & Recreation Library.)

Balcony Bridge may be spied to the east through steep, heavily wooded slopes. The large double archways of Eaglevale Arch loom just off to the west. Ice-skating was growing wildly popular at the time Central Park was being constructed, and Ladies Pond soon became popular with women skaters unwilling to skate in the presence of men. The stream below now originates from a small rocky grotto on the edge of the meadow that once was Ladies Pond. (Historic image courtesy the Collection of TheNew-York Historical Society.)

Currently built of former city lampposts, this rustic wooden bridge spans the gill as it narrows into a small stream before the cascade down to the lake. The bend in the gill just before this bridge resembles the beginnings of an oxbow lake with a lovely peninsula for a picnic. The foliage, flanking hills, and winding paths make this bridge a pleasant surprise amid a lush forested landscape.

Constructed in 1890 to accommodate the exploding residential development along Central Park West, Eaglevale Arch provided a new and necessary access to the park. The south branch of the Saw Kill stream once cascaded into Ladies Pond where Eaglevale now swoops into the park at West 77th Street just beneath the south tower of the American Museum of Natural History. Designed to carry visitors over both the bridle trail and Ladies Pond, Eaglevale Arch is the only double arch found in Central Park. A pedestrian path now passes beneath the eastern arch of Eaglevale, while the bridle trail continues under the western arch. (Historic image courtesy the Museum of the City of New York, Gift of Miss Rosmond Gilder.)

Ladies Pond was reserved for ladies-only ice-skating in the 1890s. The small body of water provided a peaceful setting for women to enjoy and practice the new national craze of ice-skating. During this era, it was thought to be inconsiderate for men to glimpse women's ankles as they changed their skates. The pond was divided into two distinctive bays, north and south of Eaglevale Arch, connected by a stream with a narrow, rocky shoreline beneath its eastern span.

The *New York Times* noted that the American Museum of Natural History was originally situated in the arsenal building at West 64th Street and Fifth Avenue. The museum had to be enlarged several times to accommodate an increasing number of exhibitions. A new building was constructed between West 79th and West 81st Streets between Eighth and Ninth Avenues on the Upper West Side. Along Azalea Walk, just to the south of Eaglevale Arch's double span, a twin pair of American elm trees thrive. The bridge inclines for 150 feet and measures 36 feet wide. The west arch is slightly more than 13 feet high above the bridle path. The east arch is 18 feet high over Ladies Pond. The pond was filled with earth in the 1930s and has served as a pedestrian path under the east arch ever since.

Nestled high atop the ramble deep in the woods, the rustic wooden Azalea Pond Bridge crosses a gentle meandering stream draining the popular bird-watching sanctuary at the head of the gill. Just upstream, casual passersby might rarely notice a small, stone slab bridge along the cascades feeding Azalea Pond. Downstream, the gill settles into a densely forested ravine passing beneath a concrete and stone pile bridge before plunging down toward the lake.

TRANSVERSE ROAD NO. 2 TO TRANSVERSE ROAD NO. 4

This vast section of the park contains the current-day reservoir named after Jacqueline Kennedy Onassis and the site of the old Croton Reservoir, in which backfill has created the Great Lawn. The name "Croton" was a strong contender for the name of Central Park until Judge Harris settled the matter in late 1856. The old Croton Reservoir, a 33-acre rectangular basin, held 180 million gallons of drinking water for thirsty New Yorkers. Water was piped through aquifers from the Croton River in Westchester County, north of Manhattan. Frederick Law Olmsted and Calvert Vaux succeeded in molding a natural landscape around the voluminous and unwieldy reservoirs. (Historic image courtesy The New York Public Library.)

Among the largest span of the masonry bridges with a height of only 12 feet and three inches, Winterdale Arch, Bridge No. 17, carries the West Drive over both the bridle trail and a pedestrian walkway just east of West 82nd Street. Constructed between 1860 and 1862, as designed by Calvert Vaux, the large yet simple 45-foot-six-inch elliptical span features slightly angled winged walls welcoming travelers through its gaping arch. The interior arch is created of Philadelphia pressed red brick laced in a diagonal pattern with crosses arranged of three Milwaukee white bricks. The grand arch was set in a winter landscape with beautiful pine trees flanking its smooth granite facings. The white-colored stone was specifically imported from Maine by boat, helping to extend the wintry feeling into the warmer seasons. It was envisioned that visitors traversing the area could experience a lush winter forest setting in the middle of Manhattan. (Historic image courtesy the Museum of the City of New York.)

Northeast of Winterdale Arch a diverse forest of pine trees was planted from around the world. The Arthur Ross Pinetum continues the tradition of Frederick Law Olmsted's original design to create a perpetual feeling of winter in this narrow corridor of Central Park. Bird-watchers traveling a circuit of prime bird-watching locations will frequent the pinetum during the chilly months when the birds may be a little easier to view in the surrounding bare deciduous trees.

The highest elevation in Central Park sits adjacent to Winterdale Arch at 141.8 feet. Summit Rock is a massive bedrock outcrop. In original park designs, Summit Rock provided views across the Hudson River to the New Jersey Palisades. Summit Rock and its immediate area were renovated in 1997 to allow classes, performers, and those who want a quiet escape to enjoy. Before Central Park was designed, the site of Summit Rock and the area surrounding it up to the pinetum was home to over 1,000 New Yorkers. This area, known as Seneca Village, contained more than 1,000 buildings, including small homes, taverns, barns, factories, and churches. In the 1830s, it was known as a well-established community. The residents were displaced when construction began on Central Park. (Historic image courtesy New York City Parks & Recreation Library.)

Missing for more than 50 years, the incredibly detailed balustrades of Winterdale Arch were reconstructed in 1994 during a comprehensive renovation by the Central Park Conservancy. A short stroll south from Winterdale Arch stands a unique open-air forum called the Delacorte Theatre. Active during summer months, the public theater and New York Shakespeare Festival schedule a variety of high-quality Shakespeare and original productions that, in keeping with park tradition, are free to the general public. The romance of an evening set adrift under the spell of a great Shakespeare in the Park performance would hardly fade from memory. A fairy-tale backdrop of Belvedere Castle high atop Vista Rock, rippling across Turtle Pond, completes the experience. Built in 1962 as merely a temporary structure, the success of the Shakespeare performances have kept this theater thriving. Performances have included *Much Ado About Nothing*, *Henry VIII*, *Agamemnon*, and *The Skin of Our Teeth*. Performers have included George C. Scott, Kevin Kline, Richard Dreyfuss, Gregory Hines, Denzel Washington, and Michelle Pfeiffer, among many others.

The narrow swath of park space along the Upper West Side border constrained between the Jacquelyn Kennedy Onassis Reservoir, Great Lawn, and Central Park West was believed too limited for extensive landscaping efforts. Frederick Law Olmsted's plan to plant a long grove of pine trees along the West Drive, north of Winterdale Arch created a perpetual winter landscape. It was an experience complete with thick forest combined with a whiff of a fresh pine scent for those traveling the West Drive by carriage and equestrians riding the bridle trail.

Greywacke Arch, Bridge No. 23, was built between 1861 and 1863 by Calvert Vaux and Jacob Wrey Mould. Its name was derived from the type of stone used in its construction, greywacke, a variety of sandstone found along the Hudson River Valley. Surrounding the spade-shaped archways, alternating shades of greywacke were used to provide a radiant pattern of stripes. Greywacke Arch was restored to its current stunning beauty by the Central Park Conservancy from 1981 through 1985. The architectural firm of Beyer, Blinder and Belle prepared plans to add substantial overhead reinforcements to better support East Drive and to further remove graffiti, paving, and vegetation while replacing iron railings, loose masonry, and dislodged stonework. (Historic image courtesy New York City Parks & Recreation Library.)

The underpass of Greywacke Arch is laid in a field of red brick with stark patterns of white brick crosses. The 56-foot pathway hosts an occasional musician while allowing pedestrians safe passage from East 79th Street under the East Drive to the Great Lawn. Benches located on the east side of the arch are most inviting to take in a view of the passersby going for a picnic or ball game on the Great Lawn or a cultural visit to the Metropolitan Museum of Art.

Calvert Vaux and Jacob Wrey Mould had the distinct honor of designing the original Metropolitan Museum of Art structure from 1870 through 1880, which soon rose above Greywacke Arch. In 1873, the *New York Times* described the construction of "a building near Eighty-second street, to be used as an art museum, the foundations for which are being now dug out."

The pointed entrance of Greywacke Arch incorporates Moorish overtones that originate from Jacob Wrey Mould's work with Owen Jones in drawing the Alhambra in Spain. An ornate gem of the park, Greywacke Arch is well-suited to its vicinity. It stands amid a rich cultural atmosphere, just south of the obelisk and leading to the Metropolitan Museum of Art, behind its glass–enclosed exhibit space. Greywacke Arch serves as a gateway to the Great Lawn, which hosts an amazing variety of free events on its 13 acres of lush green oval field. True in spirit to the noble beginnings of the park, most events are free and open to the general public, including concerts by local artists such as Paul Simon and Art Garfunkel, the Metropolitan Opera, the New York Philharmonic, and papal masses. Everyone is always invited, and hundreds of thousands attend. On the lighter side, traditional baseball games, picnics, and sunbathing on the Great Lawn are always complete with spectacular views of the surrounding New York City skyline.

Bridge No. 24 stands at the southeast entrance of the reservoir jogging track on the east side at 85th Street. This 33-foot-wide bridge provides joggers easy access to the track over the bridle path. The cast-iron structure supporting the bridge is arched, while its wood platform remains flat. This is one of three cast-iron bridges built around the reservoir to carry visitors over the bridle trail. Two trails circle the reservoir separating equestrians from joggers. The bridle trail circles the reservoir in a 1.66-mile loop. (Historic image courtesy New York City Parks & Recreation Library.)

True to how Frederick Law Olmsted envisioned the park as a place of health and fitness, joggers preparing to run the 1.58-mile track around the reservoir can be regularly found stretching and exercising along the cast-iron balustrades of this elegant southeast reservoir bridge. It is also a great spot to meet a friend or exercise partner. The bridge is neatly situated in a cozy area between Transverse Road No. 3 and a stone gatehouse for the reservoir.

Cast iron was generally less expensive and easier to craft than stone, allowing for highly detailed floral work on railings and posts.

Constructed in 1864 of cast iron and steel on the southwest shore of the reservoir, Bridge No. 27 carries a pedestrian path over the bridle trail due east of West Drive at 86th Street. The path leads north from the Great Lawn, past the Arthur Ross Pinetum, over Transverse Road No. 3, over Bridge No. 27 and the bridle trail to the reservoir jogging path. Designed by Calvert Vaux and Cornell Ironworks, it stands 10 feet and nine inches high and 38 feet and two inches wide. The balustrades and handrails of this gently arched bridge entail floral designs of leaves in spiral formations. The bridle trail splits just to the west of Bridge No. 27, allowing equestrians a choice to ride the southern perimeter of the reservoir toward Bridge No. 24 or continue north parallel to Winter Drive toward Gothic Bridge.

Consuming nearly the entire width of the park, two giant reservoirs stood between 81st and 96th Streets. The smaller, rectangular old Croton Reservoir became the Great Lawn. The significantly larger irregularly shaped reservoir, now called the Jacqueline Kennedy Onassis Reservoir, continues to serve the city today. Both had carriage drives squeezed between the bordering avenues, allowing visitors access to the northern reaches of the park. Bridge No. 27 is one of three cast-iron bridges built around the reservoir to carry visitors over the bridle trail.

In the early 1970s, a comprehensive restoration program was initiated that combined city and private funds aimed at rehabilitating a number of the bridges and archways of Central Park. Bridge No. 27 was restored in 1979. The cast iron was completely removed, and the railings and ornamentation that were still deemed usable were saved and prepared for reinstallation. Missing elements were recast with main structural steel girders and beams, which supported the new wood decking. Today it stands restored as Calvert Vaux designed it.

Bridge No. 28, known today as Gothic Bridge, was constructed by Vaux and Cornell Ironworks in 1864 of cast iron and steel. A curved 93-foot wooden walkway guided a pedestrian path over the bridle trail, providing safe passage for joggers to enter the 1.58-mile reservoir jogging track. It stands alone on the northern side of the reservoir. (Historic image courtesy New York City Parks & Recreation Library.)

Gothic Bridge derives its name from the distinct similarity in style to Middle-Age Gothic church architecture. Its abutments display paisley wisps in groups of three.

Gothic Bridge overlooks to its north 26 well-maintained clay tennis courts that buzz with daily activity during the warm seasons. Tennis gained mass popularity during the 1870s and was soon incorporated into park sports activities. Open meadows throughout the park became temporary lawn tennis courts with official lines and nets set up until a tennis house was erected by 1930. The area around Gothic Bridge, between the reservoir and Central Park Tennis Center, underwent extensive restoration work from 1999 through 2000 courtesy of the Central Park Conservancy.

Restoration plans for Gothic Bridge were underway as early as 1976. The 19th-century construction process needed to be researched, retraced, examined, and duplicated. Restoration work began in 1981 and was completed by 1983.

Bridges surrounding the reservoir were extremely important in the 19th century as hundreds of horse stables operated throughout New York City, providing for this popular recreational sport of the wealthy. The bridges allowed safe pedestrian passage for visitors above the galloping equestrians.

One of the most difficult arches to spot, 90th Street Rustic Stone Arch, known to some as Claremont Arch, was among the last arches built in 1890. Equestrians have trotted from the Claremont Riding Academy at West 89th Street and Amsterdam Avenue making their way east to the sprawling bridle trails of Central Park over the access road atop the stone arch. Established in 1892, the riding academy is the oldest continuously operating stable in the United States.

This northwest quadrant of the park was left unfinished until the vacant lots along Central Park West were filled with apartments. The demand for an access road soon became apparent as the population swelled. This was one of three arches that solved the growing demand for increased carriage access to the park, including Eaglevale Arch and 110th Street Arch. Made of Manhattan schist in rockface ashlar, this arch is slightly over eight feet high and nine feet four inches wide. In the lush seasons, the rustic stone arch is a challenge to identify as the vegetation camouflages it in deep green hues. Due to recalcitration, the 58-foot path was gated and closed to the public in 2001.

The transverse roads were the primary innovation and accounted for much of the success of the Greensward plan. Designed to enable traffic to flow crosstown through the park without being seen or heard by park visitors was a groundbreaking concept. Sunken roads several feet below grade ensured that urban traffic would not break or visually divide the length of the park. (Historic image courtesy the Collection of The New-York Historical Society.)

Transverse Road No. 2 tunnels beneath Belvedere Castle, straight through the towering 140-foot-tall Vista Rock, the second-highest elevation in the park after Summit Rock. This transverse road has three bridges and one tunnel spanning its recessed roadway. Two of its bridges carry the East Drive and West Drive separately. The other bridge is simply a pedestrian path leading from Cedar Hill to the Metropolitan Museum of Art. This road was diverted slightly north on the west side when the American Museum of Natural History expanded north to 81st Street. (Historic image courtesy The New York Public Library.)

Transverse Road No. 3 has only two bridges crossing it for each of the East and West Drives. It was excavated between the old Croton Reservoir, now the Great Lawn, and the Jacquelyn Kennedy Onassis Reservoir. Transverse Road No. 4 also has two bridges crossing it, one for each drive. It crosses the park at 96th Street between North Meadow and South Meadow.

TRANSVERSE ROAD NO. 4
TO CENTRAL PARK NORTH

This fragile woodland of cascades, a narrow lake, chirping birds, and a variety of plant life is bookended by two magnificent arches. Known as the Loch, it runs throughout the northern part of the park, connecting Glen Span Arch to Huddlestone Arch. The feeling of being worlds away in the northern parts of Upstate New York is easily experienced in this placid place. Whether bird-watching, hiking, cross-country skiing, or reading, this area is designed to alleviate the hustle and bustle of city life. It continues to serve the same purpose today. (Historic image courtesy New York City Parks & Recreation Library.)

Designed and detailed by Calvert Vaux and Jacob Wrey Mould between 1862 and 1863, Springbanks Arch, Bridge No. 25, is obscure and secluded. Located in the northern end of the North Meadow, it carries the 102nd Street surface transverse with joggers, roller bladers, and cyclists who wish to bypass the steep incline of the Harlem Hills. (Historic image courtesy The New York Public Library.)

The 17-foot-five-inch red brick passageway has two very different entrances. To the south is a set of jagged slab rock steps that bend around a stream originating from a spring. At the top of the staircase are playgrounds of the North Meadow with 12 baseball fields and six soccer fields. The north exit takes visitors on a rocky narrow passage over boulders and the current path of a tributary to Montanye's Rivulet. The surface of Springbanks Arch is made of rough stone from the Hudson River Valley, creating a semicircular archway.

The path below Springbanks Arch connecting the North Meadow to the ravine is a road less traveled. The path leading to the arch on the south side from the ravine is narrow and difficult to find as it disappears well below grade of the meadow. (Historic image courtesy New York City Parks & Recreation Library.)

The completely man-made nature of Central Park lends itself to structures necessary to deceive, similar to the backstage artistry of a good Broadway performance. This small boulder bridge passes over a stream that feeds the pool just to its north. Difficult to spot, it is dwarfed by a rocky grotto concealing a large man-made freshwater pipe replacing the stream that once fed the area. The small stone bridge is almost invisible except for the metal railings that mark its edges. The view to the north is of a meandering, rocky cascade down to the pool.

Originally Glen Span Arch was constructed between 1863 and 1865 by Calvert Vaux and Jacob Wrey Mould. Considered a rustic wooden arch with a unique wooden surface and substructure supported by a stone foundation, it carried the West Drive carriage road above, while allowing a footpath and Montanye's Rivulet to pass easily below. It was likely to have been the only arch constructed of wood to carry a carriage drive. The entire upper wooden portion of the massive arch was replaced in 1885 with light gray gneiss. (Historic image courtesy The New York Public Library.)

At the base of the falls, Montanye's Rivulet continues its journey as it flows under Glen Span Arch and into the North Woods. The sounds and sights of rushing water, rustling leaves, and falling snow highlight the changes of season, making the setting more like the Adirondacks than New York City.

Calvert Vaux's work using large, natural stones to create bridges became a fundamental form of design. He and Jacob Wrey Mould were known for their minimalism, large scale, and direct use of materials. American architecture was traveling a different path when this design element evolved in the 1860s and 1870s. The rustic stone arches of Central Park, including Huddlestone, Glen Span, and Riftstone Arches, were early examples of this pioneering style of American construction. (Historic image courtesy The New York Public Library.)

Beneath the vaulted arcade of Glen Span Arch, Bridge No. 26, a grotto swirls with the freshly fallen water from the cascade. This arch serves as a gateway to the wooded ravine of the North Woods.

This 18-foot-six-inch–high arch stands at the western entrance to the tranquility of the ravine and North Woods. A 14-foot waterfall rushes just west of Glen Span Arch and east of Rustic Wood Bridge, Bridge No. 30. (Historic image courtesy New York City Parks & Recreation Library.)

In 1866, Calvert Vaux instructed the men building Huddlestone Arch, Bridge No. 29, to only select boulders from within the park. The immense stones were huddled together by gravity and friction. No mortar, nails, or support beams were used. One of these boulders weighed over 100 tons. Unlike the other rustic stone arches in the park, the boulders of Huddlestone, constructed in 1866, appear as if a natural phenomenon created the 10-foot-high, 22-foot-wide cavelike arch.

Huddlestone Arch carries the East Drive with joggers and speeding cyclists coming off the steep mount as they gear up to approach the Harlem Hills, an incline on West Drive at the northeast corner of the park. Below the arch alongside a path, Montanye's Rivulet flows north from the Loch and a series of cascades into a creek beneath Huddlestone Arch. The sound of the water pouring over the rocks and the feel of the lush forest is likely how Calvert Vaux and Frederick Law Olmsted envisioned the area when they created this part of the park. About 90 years after the creation of Huddlestone Arch, a huge complex was built north of the arch. In the winter, it is a competitive ice hockey arena for high schools and recreational skaters. In the summer, it serves as a swimming pool, providing a cool break in the summer heat.

Spanning Montanye's Rivulet, a stone slab connects the east and west shores of the ravine at the northern end of the Loch. Simple in construction, it acts as a preview to the huddled stones of Huddlestone Arch just downstream. A gentle cascade can be viewed to the south of the stone slab bridge in this low-lying woodland valley where the sun is obscured by the forestlike overhead canopy. (Historic image courtesy New York City Parks & Recreation Library.)

Rustic Wood Bridge, Bridge No. 30, sits atop the tallest waterfall in Central Park. Mid-bridge, the long view west of the pool creates an illusion of grandeur that can only be perceived at the water level. Rising above the pool are views of apartments lining Central Park West, an unintended deviation from Frederick Law Olmsted and Calvert Vaux's original Greensward plan. The eastern view stimulates the senses with the fury of a waterfall and the rocky cliff down to the path leading under the mighty Glen Span Arch. (Historic image courtesy The New York Public Library.)

Set at the far eastern end of the pool, this rustic wood bridge marks a transformation from the romantically well-landscaped valley into the wilderness. As the flat water of the pool flows east it meets with a set of cascading boulders just before taking a 14-foot plunge.

Connected in character to the rustic stone bridges and rock work features were the numerous log constructions that Calvert Vaux built. In the early years of the park, visitors may have paused over a bridge, sat in a resting place, or took up shade in a quaint summerhouse. Most of the original pieces are now gone, yet many have been replicated. These lumber structures had a charming yet robust facade and were accepted by designers, gardeners, and architects. Most of the bridges were made of American cedar, which was plentiful in the surrounding areas of New York. These timberlike accessories provided the feeling of idealistic naturalism that set the stage for the park setting.

Montanye's Rivulet pools in this placid setting before passing beneath this small rustic bridge, Bridge No. 31. The stream cascades down toward the Loch on the east side of Bridge No. 31, touching one's sense of sound and breaking the silence of the forest. Approaching this bridge from the west, no sounds of water falling can be heard nor seen until arriving at the bridge mid-span. Crossing this rustic bridge to the north, the northern ravine is open to explore.

The grounds, drives, and walks below 102nd Street nearly all opened to New Yorkers by the end of 1863. The following two years, efforts were focused on annexing the northernmost 65 acres between 106th and 110th Streets. After four years, this rocky woodland was fully acquired, bringing the park to its current 843 acres.

Rustic Wood Bridge, Bridge No. 32, provides passage to the northern reaches of the park. This land needed less rearranging and was left to its craggy geography. The Harlem Meer, a 12-acre lake, was created on a swamp that was once part of the Harlem Creek. The ravine was planted, and a rushing waterfall was constructed.

Andrew H. Green, a member of the Central Park Board of Commissioners from 1857 to 1871, had harsh disagreements with Frederick Law Olmsted and Calvert Vaux regarding financial and political matters. Yet, it was Green who saw the brilliance of the Greensward plan and provided his support and protection that kept Central Park true to its original design. In January 1858, Green was the first commissioner to recommend a decision to extend the park from 106th Street, its original northern boundary, to 110th Street. Green was an integral player in the development of the Metropolitan Museum of Art, the American Museum of Natural History, the Central Park Menagerie, and the New York Public Library. He was also first to recommend the regions of southern Westchester (the Bronx), Kings (Brooklyn), Queens, and Richmond (Staten Island) merge with Manhattan to form the five boroughs of New York City in 1868.

At the top of the Loch sits Bridge No. 32, the last in a series of northern rustic wood bridges. A stream flows below, fed by runoff from the North Meadow, which continues its run beneath two other unnumbered stone bridges. This stream proceeds to join Montanye's Rivulet, which runs from the west side. This rustic wild setting evokes a solitude frequently found in the northern parts of New York State.

The rapid population growth into the northern reaches of New York City spurred construction of the 110th Street Arch in 1890 to provide carriage access across a deep ravine. The massive arch was added in the extreme northwest corner of the park, connecting the intersection of Central Park West and West 110th Street to a steep, mountainous section of West Drive. It was the last of three arches, including 90th Street Rustic Stone Arch and Eaglevale Arch all built in 1890 of gneiss in rockface ashlar, designed to specifically improve carriage access from the Upper West Side. Bridging a 48-foot valley, it spans 102 feet with a Tuscan-style arch that rises 16 feet above the pedestrian walkway below. Just under the arch to the east is a colorful playground equipped with a balance beam, sandbox, swings, and a cooling sprinkler for hot days.

Lion's Head Rock, the cliff, and the Great Hill are all to the south and tower more than a 100 feet over the 110th Street Arch. The oldest structure in the park, Blockhouse No. 1, stands atop the cliff and was used as a northern lookout post with a view of Long Island Sound, dating back to the War of 1812. After the attack on Long Island Sound at Stonington, Connecticut, the city realized it needed to defend itself. Three blockhouses were built on what is now known as Morningside Heights. Blockhouse No. 1 is the only fort on Manhattan surviving from the war.

INDEX

Bibliography

"Andrew H. Green and Central Park." *Illustrated Weekly Magazine*. October 10, 1897, SM6.

Architects Report. January 1858.

Barlow, Elizabeth. *Frederick Law Olmsted's New York*. New York: Praeger Publishers, 1972.

Berman, John S. *The Museum of the City of New York Portraits of America: Central Park*. New York: Barnes and Noble Publishing Inc., 2003.

Beveridge, Charles E., and David Schuyler, ed. *The Papers of Frederick Law Olmsted*. Baltimore: The Johns Hopkins University Press, 1983.

Board of Commissioners of the Central Park. Eleventh Annual Report. New York: William C. Bryant and Company, December 1867.

———. Fifth Annual Report. New York: William C. Bryant and Company, January 1862.

———. First Annual Report on the Improvement of the Central Park. New York: Chas. Baker, January 1857.

———. Ninth Annual Report. New York: William C. Bryant and Company, December 1865.

———. Seventh Annual Report. New York: William C. Bryant and Company, December 1863.

———. Sixth Annual Report. New York: William C. Bryant and Company, January 1863.

———. Third Annual Report. New York: William C. Bryant and Company, January 1860.

———. Twelfth Annual Report. New York: Evening Post Steam Presses, December 1868.

Bryant, William Cullen. "The Parks of London.—The Police." In *Letters of a Traveller: Notes of Things Seen in Europe and America*. Project Gutenberg, 2004. http://www.gutenberg.org/files/11013/11013-h/11013-h.htm#ch21.

Chadwick, George F. *The Park and the Town*. Westminster, England: Architectural Press, 1966.

Colbert, George, and Guenter Vollath. *Maps of Central Park and Profile of Central Park and Manhattan Island and its Parks*. 1994.

Cook, Clarence C. *A Description of the New York Central Park*. New York: Benjamin Blom, Inc., 1979.

Department of Parks of the City of New York. Annual Report. 1908.

Dunlap, David W. "Small Scale, Great Beauty: The Bridges of Central Park." *New York Times*, July 15, 1991, C1.

Dunning, Jennifer. "New Tour Spans Cast-Iron Bridges of Central Park." *New York Times*, June 6, 1980, C1.

Fein, Albert. *Frederick Law Olmsted and the American Environmental Tradition*. New York: George Braziller, Publisher, 1972.

———. *Landscape into Cityscape: Frederick Law Olmsted's Plans for a Greater New York City*. York, PA: Maple Press Company/Cornell University Press, 1967.

Greywacke Arch. New York: Beyer, Blinder and Bele, 1981. Architectural drawing.

http://www.centralparknyc.org

http://www.ci.columbia.edu

http://www.elizabethbarlowrogers.com

http://www.gardenvisit.com

http://www.greenswardparks.org

http://www.gutenberg.org

http://www.library.cornell.edu

http://www.nycgovparks.org

http://www.potomachorse.com

Kinkead, Eugene. *Central Park 1857–1995: The Birth, Decline and Renewal of a National Treasure*. New York: W. W. Norton and Company, *c.* 1995.

Kowsky, Francis R. *Country, Park and City: The Architecture and Life of Calvert Vaux*. New York: Oxford University Press, Inc., 1998.

McGee, Robert M., Esther Mipaas, and Henry Hope Reed. "Central Park Guide: A Book of Bridges and Arches." Illustrated by Ronald Rife and Joseph LoGuirato. *New York Times*, September 16, 1990, R1.

Miller, Sarah Cedar. *Central Park: An American Masterpiece*. New York: Harry N. Abrams, Inc., 2003.

New York Daily Times, "A Name for Our New Park," February, 8, 1856, 4.

New York Daily Times, "The Central Park," July 9, 1856, 4.

New York Daily Times, "The New Parks," August 9, 1853, 4.

New York Times, "Calvert Vaux Was Drowned: Body of the Landscape Architect Found in Gravesend Bay—Probably Fell from a Pier," November 22, 1895, 1.

New York Times, "The Central Park," April 26, 1859, 4.

New York Times, "Central Park—Its Present Aspect and Proposed Improvements—The Museum—New Drives, Walks, and Bridges," April 5, 1873, 4.

New York Times, "Central Park: Map and Description of the Plan which Took the $2,000 Prize for the Central Park," May 1, 1858, 1.

New York Times, "Hints for the Park Commissioners," August 25, 1871, 4.

New York Times, "Manhattan's Central Park: An Island Refuge within an Island," October 25, 1953, X31.

New York Times, "Parks, Places and Squares: Two Ways of Spending Public Money—The Startling Record of Sweeney, Hilton and Fields—What the People Gain by a New Park Commission," December 22, 1871, 1.

New York Times, "Restoration: Central Park," October 7, 1984, SM102.

New York Times, "Restored Bow Bridge Reopens to Pedestrians," September 24, 1974, 45.

New York Times, "Sunday in Central Park," June 15, 1874, 8.

Reed, Henry Hope, Robert M. McGee, and Esther Mipaas. Illustrated by Ronald Rife and Joseph LoGuirato. *Bridges of Central Park*. New York: Greensward Foundation, Inc., 1990.

Reed, Henry Hope, and Victor Laredo. *Central Park: A Photographic Guide*. New York: Dover Publications, Inc., 1979.

Rogers, Elizabeth Barlow. *Rebuilding Central Park: A Management and Restoration Plan*. Cambridge, MA: The MIT Press, 1987.

Rosenzweig, Roy, and Elizabeth Blackmar. *The Park and the People: A History of Central Park*. Ithaca, NY: Cornell University Press, 1992.

Seltzer, Thomas, and the Central Park Association. *The Central Park*. New York: Thomas Seltzer and the Central Park Association, 1926.

Vaux, Calvert. "A Plea for the Artistic Unity of Central Park." *New York Times*, August 27, 1879, 5.

W., A.V. Letter to the editor. *New York Daily Times*, June 4, 1853, 3.

ACROSS AMERICA, PEOPLE ARE DISCOVERING SOMETHING WONDERFUL. *THEIR HERITAGE.*

Arcadia Publishing is the leading local history publisher in the United States. With more than 3,000 titles in print and hundreds of new titles released every year, Arcadia has extensive specialized experience chronicling the history of communities and celebrating America's hidden stories, bringing to life the people, places, and events from the past. To discover the history of other communities across the nation, please visit:

www.arcadiapublishing.com

Customized search tools allow you to find regional history books about the town where you grew up, the cities where your friends and family live, the town where your parents met, or even that retirement spot you've been dreaming about.

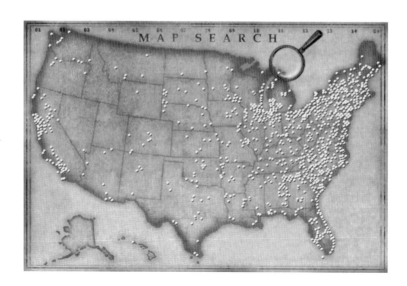